Defusing DISHARMONY

Seeking Restoration When Christians Collide

Charles R. Swindoll

Insight for Living

DEFUSING DISHARMONY
By Charles R. Swindoll

Charles R. Swindoll has devoted his life to the clear, practical teaching and application of God's Word and His grace. Chuck currently is the senior pastor of Stonebriar Community Church in Frisco, Texas, but his listening audience extends far beyond this local church body. As a leading program in Christian broadcasting, *Insight for Living* airs in major Christian radio markets around the world, reaching people groups in languages they can understand. Chuck's extensive writing ministry has also served the body of Christ worldwide, and his leadership as president and now chancellor of Dallas Theological Seminary has helped prepare and equip a new generation for ministry.

Copyright © 1992, 2010 by Charles R. Swindoll, Inc.

All rights reserved worldwide under international copyright conventions. No portion of *Defusing Disharmony* may be reproduced, stored in a retrieval system, or transmitted in any form or by any means—electronic, mechanical, photocopy, recording, or any other—except for brief quotations in printed reviews, without the prior written permission of the publisher. Inquiries should be addressed to Insight for Living, Rights and Permissions, Post Office Box 251007, Plano, Texas, 75025-1007 or sent by e-mail to rights@insight.org.

Published By: IFL Publishing House, A Division of Insight for Living
Post Office Box 251007, Plano, Texas 75025-1007

The text of this booklet was taken from chapter 11 "Defusing Disharmony" of Charles R. Swindoll's book, *Laugh Again: Experience Outrageous Joy* (Dallas: Word Publishing, 1992) 175–187. Copyright © 1992 by Charles R. Swindoll, Inc.

Editor in Chief: Cynthia Swindoll, President, Insight for Living
Executive Vice President: Wayne Stiles, Th.M., D.Min.,
    Dallas Theological Seminary
Theological Editor: Michael J. Svigel, Th.M., Ph.D.,
    Dallas Theological Seminary
Copy Editors: Jim Craft, M.A., English, Mississippi College
    Melanie Munnell, M.A., Humanities,
    The University of Texas at Dallas
Project Supervisor, Creative Ministries: Cari Harris, B.A. Journalism,
    Grand Canyon University
Project Coordinator, Communications: Kim Gibbs,
    Trinity Valley Community College, 1991–1993
Proofreader: Paula McCoy, B.A., English,
    Texas A&M University–Commerce
Cover Designer: Kari Pratt, B.A., Commercial Art,
    Southwestern Oklahoma State University
Production Artist: Nancy Gustine, B.F.A., Advertising Art,
    North Texas State University
Back Cover Photo: David Edmondson

Unless otherwise identified, Scripture quotations are from the *New American Standard Bible*® (NASB). Copyright © 1960, 1962, 1963, 1968, 1971, 1972, 1973, 1975, 1977, 1995 by The Lockman Foundation, La Habra, California. All rights reserved. Used by permission. (www.lockman.org)

Scripture quotations marked (LB) are taken from *The Living Bible*. Copyright © 1971 by Tyndale House Publishers, Inc. Wheaton, IL 60189 USA. All rights reserved. Used by permission.

Scripture quotations marked (MSG) are from *The Message*. Copyright © 1993, 1994, 1995, 1996, 2000, 2001, 2002 by Eugene H. Peterson. All rights reserved. Used by permission of NavPress Publishing Group.

Scripture quotations marked (NIV) are taken from the *Holy Bible, New International Version*®. *NIV*®. Copyright © 1973, 1978, 1984 by International Bible Society. All rights reserved. Used by permission of Zondervan.

An effort has been made to locate sources and obtain permission where necessary for the quotations used in this booklet. In the event of any unintentional omission, a modification will gladly be incorporated in future printings.

ISBN: 978-1-57972-803-8
Printed in the United States of America

Defusing DISHARMONY

| Seeking Restoration
When Christians Collide |

A Letter from Chuck

One of the marks of spiritual maturity is the ability to disagree without becoming disagreeable. Because of this, you might think that the church would be the one place where we could find acceptance, tact, room for disagreement, and open discussion—all centered on Christ and God's Word.

The reality? Many ministries survive on the ragged edge of upheaval. If the fuse of disharmony is allowed to burn, whispered criticisms will turn into shouting matches. The squabbles of a few divisive spirits can lead to a divided church. If the controversy is not defused, the church will explode due to the unresolved conflict. And in the aftermath, harsh words stick like pieces of shrapnel in the brain.

The fact is, disagreements—whether between churches or between members of the same church—are inevitable. Even godly Christians disagree. This is why the Bible itself records interpersonal conflicts among God's people. But the same Bible that reports conflict also gives principles on how to defuse it.

Many of us need to come to terms with lingering, nagging issues that are simmering on the back burner of our minds and with other issues that are boiling violently, ready to explode. Some are standing back, watching people fan the flames of controversy, unsure of how or when — or even *whether or not* — to intervene. My hope is that the message in this booklet will help you discover that you can be part of the healing process.

You *can* help defuse disharmony . . . and I believe you will.

With my best hopes,

Chuck Swindoll

Charles R. Swindoll

Defusing Disharmony

Seeking Restoration When Christians Collide

In a parable she titles "A Brawling Bride," Karen Mains paints a vivid scene, describing a suspenseful moment in a wedding ceremony. Down front stands the groom in a spotless tuxedo—handsome, smiling, full of anticipation, shoes shined, every hair in place, anxiously awaiting the presence of his bride. All attendants are in place, looking joyful and attractive. The magical moment finally arrives as the pipe organ reaches full crescendo and the stately wedding march begins.

Everyone rises and looks toward the door for their first glimpse of the bride. Suddenly there is a horrified gasp. The wedding party is shocked. The groom stares in embarrassed disbelief. Instead of a lovely woman dressed in elegant white, smiling behind a lace veil, the bride is limping down the aisle. Her dress is soiled and torn. Her leg seems twisted. Ugly cuts and bruises cover her bare arms. Her nose is bleeding, one eye is purple and swollen, and her hair is disheveled.

"Does not this handsome groom deserve better than this?" asks the author. And then the clincher: "Alas, His bride, THE CHURCH, has been fighting again!"[1]

Calling them (and us) "the church," the apostle Paul writes to the Ephesians:

> Christ loved the church and gave himself up for her to make her holy, cleansing her by the washing with water through the word, and to present her to himself as a radiant church, without stain or wrinkle or any other blemish, but holy and blameless.
> (Ephesians 5:25–27 NIV)

Wonderful plan . . . but hardly a realistic portrayal. I mean, can you imagine what the wedding pictures would look like if Christ claimed His bride, the church, *today*? Try to picture Him standing next to His brawling bride. It is one thing for us to survive the blows of a world that is hostile to the things of Christ, but to be in disharmony with one another, fighting and arguing among ourselves—unthinkable.

Puritan Thomas Brookes once penned these words: "For wolves to worry lambs is no wonder, but for lambs to worry one another, this is unnatural and monstrous."[2]

Unthinkable and unnatural though it may seem, the bride has been brawling for centuries. We get along for a little while and then we are back at each others' throats. After a bit we make up, walk in wonderful harmony for a few days, then we turn on one another. We can switch from friend to fiend in a matter of moments.

In a *Peanuts* cartoon, Lucy says to Snoopy: "You know, there are times when you really bug me! But I must admit there are also times when I feel like giving you a hug . . ."

Snoopy replies: "That's the way I am . . . bugable and hugable!"[3]

And so it is with us and our relationships within the ranks of God's family. I'm not referring to the variety of our personalities, gifts, tastes, and preferences—that's healthy. The Master made us like that. It's our mistreatment of each other, the infighting, the angry assaults, the verbal misrepresentations, the choosing of sides, the stubborn wills, the childish squabbles. An objective onlooker who watches us from a distance could wonder how and why some of us call ourselves Christians. "Well," you ask, "must we always agree?" No, absolutely not. But my question is this: Why can't we be *agreeable*? What is it that makes us so ornery and nitpicking in our attitudes? Why so many petty fights and ugly quarrels? Why so little acceptance and tolerance? Aren't we given the direct command to "preserve the unity of the Spirit in the bond of peace" (Ephesians 4:3)? What makes Christ's bride forget those words and have so many verbal brawls?

Analyzing Conflict's Cause and Extent

James asked similar questions back in the first century—which tells us that disharmony is not solely a twenty-first-century malady. Even back in the days when life was simple and everyone's pace was slower, there were squabbles.

> What is the source of quarrels and conflicts among you? Is not the source your pleasures that wage war in your members? You lust and do not have; so you commit murder. You are envious and cannot obtain; so you fight and quarrel. You do not have because you do not ask. You ask and do not receive, because

> you ask with wrong motives, so that
> you may spend it on your pleasures.
> (James 4:1–3)

James never was the type to beat around the bush. With penetrating honesty he asks and answers the critical question. The terms he uses are extremely descriptive: "quarrels and conflicts." The first term is from the Greek word for "war." It conveys a scene of broad and bloody hostility between opposing parties. The second represents smaller skirmishes, local and limited battles, even a chronic state of disharmony. During World War II there were two massive "theaters" of warfare, vast territories on opposite sides of the United States: the European theater of war and the Pacific theater of war. Within both, numerous skirmishes and individual battles took place. That is the idea here.

The same can be seen to this day within the ranks of religion. England and Ireland have sustained their territorial and denominational "quarrel" for centuries. People on both sides were killed and crippled by real bombs and real bullets. Less bloody perhaps, but no less real are the denominational quarrels in our own land—fights and splits within the ranks. Seminaries quarrel as one theological position takes up arms against another. The disputes appear civil and sophisticated as each side publishes its position in journals and books, but behind the veil of intellectualism is a great deal of hostility.

And then there are those "conflicts" between local churches as well as among members of the same church. Small, petty battles . . . arguments, power struggles, envyings, catty comments, silent standoffs, and even lawsuits between members of the body of Christ. These may not be on the national news, but they can get ugly.

A pastor from another state recently told me that some of the members of his board of elders had not spoken to one another for over a year. A concerned board member from a different church in another state said he had recently resigned because he had gotten exhausted from doing nothing but "putting out fires" and "trying to keep church members happy." His particular church had been through two major splits in the past seven years over reasons that would make you smile and shake your head in disbelief. Such are the "conflicts among us."

Why We Have Them

James points to "the source" as he addresses the issue. His answer may seem strange: "Is not the source your pleasures that wage war in your members?" (James 4:1).

"Pleasures" doesn't sound very hostile, does it? Maybe not in our English language, but the Greek word is the one from which we get "hedonism." It means the strong desire to get what one does not have, which includes the idea of satisfying oneself . . . the passion to get what one wants, regardless. Such an intense craving drives us to shameful and selfish actions. As James puts it, such pleasures lead us to "wage war"—*strateuo*—from which we get "strategy." Our desire to get what we want prompts us to strategize: to put a plan in motion that will result in *my* getting *my* way.

Is this a determined effort? Look again at what James writes:

> You lust and do not have; so you commit murder. You are envious and cannot obtain; so you fight and quarrel. You do not have because you do not ask. (James 4:2)

I'd call that determined! If it calls for a fight, *fight*! If it means an argument, *argue*! If it will require getting other people to back me up, *enlist*!

If stronger words will help me reach my objective and get what I want, *murder*!

I realize we don't carry weapons to church—not literally. That is not necessary, since the muscle behind our teeth is always ready to launch its killing missiles. We may not bring blood from another's body, but we certainly know how to make him or her squirm and hopefully surrender. And we never admit it is because we are selfish or because we crave our own way—there's always a principle at stake or a cause worth fighting for that's bigger than personalities. Sure, sure.

I realize that on a few occasions conflicts will arise. There *are* those times when it is essential to stand one's ground and refuse to compromise biblical principles. But more often than not the nasty infighting among us is embarrassingly petty. And, unfortunately, the world has a field day watching us fight and quarrel for the silliest of reasons.

Ways We Express Our Disharmony

Rationalizing our wrong attitudes and actions, we Christians will go to amazing lengths to get our way. The history of the church is strewn with the litter of battle. I repeat, some of those fights were unselfish and necessary. To have backed away would have meant compromising convictions clearly set forth in the Scriptures. But more often than not the "quarrels and conflicts" have expressed themselves in personal power plays, political maneuvering, strong-minded and selfish parishioners determined to get their own way, stubborn pastors who intimidate and bully others, unbending and tightfisted board members who refuse to listen to reason and, yes, those who seem to delight in stirring up others through rumor and gossip. It's just a mess! Sometimes I wonder how the Shepherd puts up with us. We can be such wayward, stubborn sheep! And to think He sees it all—each and every cutting word or ugly act—yet loves us still. Only because of His grace are we able to continue on.

Marshall Shelley, in his book *Well-Intentioned Dragons*, talks about disharmony in the church from another perspective. Sometimes it is from folks who don't necessarily mean to be difficult, but they are.

> Dragons, of course, are fictional beasts—monstrous reptiles with lion's claws, a serpent's tail, bat wings, and scaly skin. They exist only in the imagination.

But there are dragons of a different sort, decidedly real. In most cases, though not always, they do not intend to be sinister; in fact, they're usually quite friendly. But their charm belies their power to destroy.

Within the church, they are often sincere, well-meaning saints, but they leave ulcers, strained relationships, and hard feelings in their wake. They don't consider themselves difficult people. They don't sit up nights thinking of ways to be nasty. Often they are pillars of the community—talented, strong personalities, deservingly respected—but for some reason, they undermine the ministry of the church. They are not naturally rebellious or pathological; they are loyal church members, convinced they're serving God, but they wind up doing more harm than good.

They can drive pastors crazy . . . or out of the church.

Some dragons are openly critical. They are the ones who accuse you of being (pick one) too spiritual, not spiritual enough, too dominant, too laid back, too narrow, too loose, too structured, too disorganized, or ulterior in your motives.

These criticisms are painful because they are largely unanswerable. How can you defend yourself and maintain a spirit of peace? How can you possibly prove the purity of your motives? Dragons make it hard to disagree without being disagreeable.

Relationships are both the professional and personal priority for pastors—getting along with people is an essential element of any ministry—and when relationships are vandalized by critical dragons, many pastors feel like failures. Politicians are satisfied with 51 percent of the constituency behind them; pastors, however, feel the pain when one vocal member becomes an opponent.

Sightings of these dragons are all too common. As one veteran pastor says, "Anyone who's been in ministry more than an hour and a half knows the wrath of a dragon." Or, as Harry Ironside described it, "Wherever there's light, there's bugs."[4]

Looking through the Keyhole of a First-Century Church

I would be a lot more discouraged about the problem of disharmony among believers if I didn't remember that it has been around since the church began. Those early churches were anything but pockets of perfection. Christians in places like Corinth and Galatia, Rome and Thessalonica had their troubles just like those living in towns and cities all around our world today. Even Philippi—as fine a group of Jesus People as they were—had their own skirmishes, one of which Paul pinpointed in his letter to them.

> Therefore, my beloved brethren whom I long to see, my joy and crown, in this way stand firm in the Lord, my beloved. I urge Euodia and I urge Syntyche to live in harmony in the Lord. Indeed, true companion, I ask you also to help these women who have shared my struggle in the cause of the gospel, together with Clement also and the rest of my

> fellow workers, whose names are in the book of life. (Philippians 4:1–3)

In his typical fashion, Paul starts with a general principle before he addresses a specific concern; then he wraps things up as he makes a request. Behind it all is his unspoken desire that the Philippians defuse the disharmony and begin to rejoice in diversity. When disharmony persists, the first thing to go is the sweetest sound that can be heard in a church—laughter. Perhaps it had been too long since the Philippians had enjoyed the presence of one another. Paul's hope is that once this difficulty is cleared up, their joy might return.

A Primary Principle

Solving problems that grow out of disharmony among believers calls for a return to standing firm in the things of the Lord, not satisfying self.

> Therefore, my beloved brethren whom I long to see, my joy and crown, in this way stand firm in the Lord, my beloved. (Philippians 4:1)

Earlier in the letter Paul had written:

> Only conduct yourselves in a manner worthy of the gospel of

> Christ, so that whether I come and see you or remain absent, I will hear of you that you are standing firm in one spirit, with one mind striving together for the faith of the gospel. (Philippians 1:27)

Actually, the idea of standing firm is one of the apostle's favorite topics. For example:

> Stand firm in the faith. (1 Corinthians 16:13)

> Keep standing firm. (Galatians 5:1)

> Now we really live, if you stand firm in the Lord. (1 Thessalonians 3:8)

> So then, brethren, stand firm. (2 Thessalonians 2:15)

Why place such an emphasis on standing firm in the Lord? What's the big deal? Let me suggest to you that it is one of the most foundational principles of maintaining harmony:

STANDING FIRM IN THE LORD

PRECEDES

RELATING WELL IN THE FAMILY

What would standing firm include? Following Christ's teachings. Respecting His Word. Modeling His priorities. Loving His people. Seeking and carrying out His will. It has been my observation that those who are committed to these things have little difficulty relating well to other members of God's family. Not surprisingly the very next issue Paul brings up has to do with two in the church at Philippi who needed to "live in harmony" with one another. But before I go into that, this might be a good time for you to ask yourself, "Am I one who stands firm *in the Lord*?" Other options create havoc: Standing firm *for what I want* . . . or standing firm *in honor of tradition* . . . or standing firm *with a couple of my friends*." Unquestionably, those three positions represent the antithesis of "standing firm in the Lord."

A Relational Need

Having stated the principle, Paul puts his finger on the specific conflict at Philippi. He even names names.

> I urge Euodia and I urge Syntyche to live in harmony in the Lord. (Philippians 4:2)

Let me mention several observations:

1. These are two women in the church at Philippi (feminine names).

2. They are mentioned nowhere else in the Scriptures.

3. The specific details of their dispute are not explained.

4. Paul's counsel is to urge them toward harmony: "I urge . . . I urge." (He neither rebukes them nor pontificates.)

5. He appeals to their conscience . . . their hearts (intrinsic motivation).

I am just as impressed with what Paul does not do.

He does not spell out a step-by-step process; that was for the two women to work out on their own. Equally impressive, he does not pull rank by adding a warning or a threat, like, "I'll give you two weeks to clear this up," or "If you don't straighten up, I will . . ."

Paul handled the matter with dignity and grace. While he was deeply concerned ("I urge . . . I urge"), he did not attempt to take charge of the situation from a distance. If anyone is tempted to think Paul was too passive or should have said more, a quick reading of other renderings may help:

- "I plead with . . . I plead with . . ." (NIV)

- "Please, please, with the Lord's help, quarrel no more—be friends again" (LB)

- "I urge Euodia and Syntyche to iron out their differences and make up. God doesn't want his children holding grudges." (MSG)

By repeating the verb ("I urge . . . I urge"), Paul leaves the impression that there was fault on both sides. In fact, the Vulgate, the Latin version of Scripture, uses different verbs in the appeal, which seem to emphasize mutual wrong.

I have seldom seen an exception to this: When disharmony arises between two people or two groups, there is some measure of fault on both sides. The road leading to a breakdown in harmony is never a one-way street. Both parties must be encouraged to see each other's fault, each other's failure . . . and meet on common ground with a mutual willingness to listen and to change.

And what is that common ground? The statement Paul makes includes the answer: "live in harmony in the Lord." Just as we are to "stand firm" in Him, so are we to find agreement in Him. Both sides need to make Him their focus if a solution is ever going to be found. It is as if Paul, the Apostle of Grace, is saying, "It is important that both release their grudge and state their forgiveness and adopt the same attitude as their Lord when He unselfishly came from heaven to earth to be our Savior. Only then will there be renewed harmony."

One more thought before moving on. Everything we know of these two women is: They quarreled. Down through the centuries the only answer that could be given to the question: "Who were Euodia and Syntyche?" has been "They were two women from Philippi who lived in disharmony." That prompts me to ask you: If *your* life were to be summed up in a single statement, what would that statement be?

An Affirming Request

Occasionally a dispute is so deep and long-standing that it calls for a third party — an objective, unprejudiced arbitrator — to come between those in conflict to help bring restoration. That is Paul's request here:

> Indeed, true companion, I ask you also to help these women who have shared my struggle in the cause of the gospel, together with Clement also and the rest of my fellow workers, whose names are in the book of life. (Philippians 4:3)

All sorts of suggestions have been made as to the identity of the one called "true companion." One scholar suggested Barnabas. If so, why didn't Paul call him by name? Another said it could have been Epaphroditus. But, again, one wonders why he would have been called by name earlier yet referred to as "true companion" here. A curious suggestion has been a person named Sunzugos, which is the Greek transliteration of "companion." One fanciful idea is that the person was one of their husbands (I doubt that either husband would have relished that role) . . . another, that it was Paul's wife!

The name of the mediator is not nearly as important as the help that he or she could bring ("help these women"). Why did this mean so much to Paul that he included it in his letter? Because these women were important. They had "shared in the struggle" with Paul, and they belonged to the same spiritual family. Their clash was hurting the fellowship among the

Christians at Philippi, so it needed resolution . . . soon. The bride needed to stop brawling!

Someone has said that Christians trying to live in close harmony is the next thing to impossible. The scene is not unlike the old forest folktale where two porcupines were huddled close together on a cold, cold night up in northern Canada. The closer they got to stay warm, the more their quills pricked each other, making it virtually impossible for them to remain side by side. Silently, they scooted apart. Before long, they were shivering in the wintry gale, so they came back together. Soon both were poking and jabbing each other . . . so they separated again. Same story . . . same result. Their action was like a slow-moving, monotonous dance—back and forth, back and forth.

Those two women in Philippi were like the Canadian porcupines; they needed each other, but they kept needling each other. Unfortunately, the disruptive dance of disharmony did not stop in that first-century church.

May I speak to you heart-to-heart, as friend-to-friend, before ending this booklet? In all honesty, have my words opened an old wound that has never healed? Did the imaginary scene of a brawling bride bring back a few ugly memories of an unresolved conflict in your past . . . or maybe several of them? Is there someone you continue to blame for the hurt you had to endure, bringing pain that never got reconciled? If so, do you have any idea how much emotional energy you are burning up nursing that wound? And while I'm asking questions: Are you aware of the joy-stealing effect an unforgiving spirit is having on your life? If your bitterness is deep enough, you've virtually stopped living. It is no wonder you have also stopped laughing!

Please listen to me. *It is not worth it.* You need to come to terms with this lingering, nagging issue *now.* The peace and contentment and joy that could be yours are draining away, like water down the drain of an unplugged bathtub. It is time for you to call a halt to the dispute; the disharmony must be defused. But it won't happen automatically. You are an essential part of the healing equation. You must do something about it.

Start by telling God how much it hurts and that you need Him to help you to forgive the offense. If you have a friend who is close enough to you to help you work your way through the process, reach out and say so. Get rid of all the poison of built-up anger and pour out all the acid of long-term resentment. Your objective is clear: Fully forgive the offender. Once that is done, you will discover that you no longer rehearse the ugly scenes in your mind. The revengeful desire to get back and get even will wane, and in its now-empty space will come such an outpouring of relief and a new spirit of joy that you won't feel like the same person. That deep frown on your brow and those long lines on your face will slowly disappear. And before too long you will get reacquainted with a sound you haven't made for months, maybe years. It is called laughter.

A resentful, unforgiving spirit and a carefree, happy heart never existed in the same body. Until you take care of the former you won't be able to enjoy the latter.

Considering the Lessons This Teaches Us...

I can think of at least four practical lessons we have learned from the things we have been considering.

1. Clashes will continue to occur. I wish I could promise you otherwise, but as long as depravity pollutes humanity, we can forget about a conflict-free environment. So, don't be surprised when another skirmish breaks out.

2. Not all conflicts are wrong. Not all disagreements require reconciliation. As I recall, it was Jesus who said that He brings "a sword" into certain relationships. Occasionally it is right to be defiant and to fight. When critical biblical lines are drawn and the issues at stake have nothing to do with personal preferences or individual personalities, surrendering to a cause that would lead to wrong is wrong.

3. If the disagreement *should* be resolved and *could* be resolved but is not, then stubbornness and selfishness are at the core. We may be adults in age and height, but we can be awfully childish in attitude. Come on, give in. To persist in this lack of harmony brings hurts far greater than the small radius of your relationship.

4. Should you be the companion needed to assist in the reconciliation, remember the threefold objective:

- The ultimate goal: Restoration (not discipline)

- The overall attitude: Grace (not force)

- The common ground: Christ (not logic or the church or tradition or your will)

There is something magnanimous about the name of Jesus that softens our attitudes and defuses disharmony. Somehow the insertion of His name makes it inappropriate to maintain a fighting spirit.

The truth of that was underscored when I read of something that happened more than one hundred years ago.

Charles H. Spurgeon, Baptist minister of London, England, had a pastor-friend, Dr. Newman Hall, who wrote a book titled *Come to Jesus*. Another preacher published an article in which he ridiculed Hall, who bore it patiently for a little while. But when the article gained popularity, Hall sat down and wrote a letter of protest. His answer was full of retaliatory invectives that outdid anything in the article that attacked him. Before mailing the letter, Hall took it to Spurgeon for his opinion.

Spurgeon read it carefully then, handing it back, asserted it was excellent and that the writer of the article deserved it all. "But," he added, "it just lacks one thing." After a pause Spurgeon continued, "Underneath your signature you ought to write the words, 'Author of *Come to Jesus*.'"

The two godly men looked at each other for a few minutes. Then Hall tore the letter to shreds.[5]

We Are Here for You

If you desire to find out more about knowing God and His plan for you in the Bible, contact us. Insight for Living provides staff pastors who are available for free written correspondence or phone consultation. These seminary-trained and seasoned counselors have years of experience and are well-qualified guides for your spiritual journey.

Please feel welcome to contact your regional Pastoral Ministries by using the information below:

United States
Insight for Living
Pastoral Ministries
Post Office Box 269000
Plano, Texas 75026-9000
USA
972-473-5097, Monday through Friday,
8:00 a.m. – 5:00 p.m. Central time
www.insight.org/contactapastor

INSIGHT FOR LIVING
Post Office Box 269000 · Plano, Texas 75026-9000
800-772-8888 · 972-473-5000 · +1-972-473-5136
www.insightworld.org · www.insight.org

Canada

Insight for Living Canada
Pastoral Ministries
Post Office Box 2510
Vancouver, BC V6B 3W7
CANADA
1-800-663-7639
info@insightforliving.ca

Australia, New Zealand, and South Pacific

Insight for Living Australia
Pastoral Care
Post Office Box 443
Boronia, VIC 3155
AUSTRALIA
1 300 467 444

United Kingdom and Europe

Insight for Living United Kingdom
Pastoral Care
PO Box 553
Dorking
RH4 9EU
UNITED KINGDOM
0800 915 9364
pastoralcare@insightforliving.org.uk

Endnotes

1. Karen Mains, *The Key to a Loving Heart* (Elgin, Ill.: David C. Cook, 1979), 143–44.

2. Thomas Brookes, *The Golden Treasure of Puritan Quotations*, ed. I. D. E. Thomas (Chicago: Moody Press, 1975), 304.

3. Charles M. Schulz, *Peanuts*, © United Features Syndicate, Inc. Used by permission.

4. Marshall Shelley, *Well-Intentioned Dragons* (Waco, Tex.: Word Books/CTi, Copyright © 1985), 11–12.

5. Leslie B. Flynn, *You Don't Have to Go It Alone* (Denver: Accent Books, 1981), 117.

Ordering Information

If you would like to order additional copies of *Defusing Disharmony* or order other Insight for Living resources, please contact the office that serves you.

United States
Insight for Living
Post Office Box 269000
Plano, Texas 75026-9000
USA
1-800-772-8888
(Monday through Friday,
7:00 a.m.–7:00 p.m. Central time)
www.insight.org
www.insightworld.org

Canada
Insight for Living Canada
Post Office Box 2510
Vancouver, BC V6B 3W7
CANADA
1-800-663-7639
www.insightforliving.ca

Australia, New Zealand, and South Pacific
Insight for Living Australia
Post Office Box 443
Boronia, VIC 3155
AUSTRALIA
1 300 467 444
www.insight.asn.au

United Kingdom and Europe
Insight for Living United Kingdom
PO Box 553
Dorking
RH4 9EU
UNITED KINGDOM
0800 915 9364
www.insightforliving.org.uk

Other International Locations
International constituents may contact the U.S. office through our Web site (www.insightworld.org), mail queries, or by calling +1-972-473-5136.